The Power of Thought

By Henry Thomas Hamblin

ISBN 0-9792665-9-9

Printed in the United States of America

INTRODUCTION

You are the architect of your own life: it is yours to make or to mar.
By the power of thoughts you are building; are you building aright?

The power of thought, as Emerson says, is a spiritual power. It is the greatest power that man has at his disposal. The world today is in its present state simply as a result of mankind's collective thinking; each nation is in its present state of either peace and prosperity, or poverty, murder and anarchy, simply as a result of its thinking as a nation; and each individual is what he is, and his life is what it is, and his circumstances are what they are, simply as results of his thoughts.

What a man thinks, he becomes; what a man thinks is the mainspring of all his actions; what a man thinks attracts to him his circumstances and environment; what a man thinks determines what type of friends and companions will gather around him; what a man thinks decides whether he shall be happy or miserable, successful or unsuccessful, healthy or unhealthy, prosperous or poverty-stricken, hated or loved. What a man thinks either builds up his character or pulls it down.

What a man thinks can overcome fate or strengthen it, can bring him into alignment with his glorious destiny, or make him an outcast and a wanderer in desert places.

Indeed, there is no limit to the power of thought, because it is a spiritual power of intense potency.

It is the power which distinguishes man from the brute, it is the power by which he can mount up to God, it is the power which can make the unsuccessful successful in the battle of life, it is the power which can make the loftiest achievement possible, it is the power by which difficulties can be overcome, disadvantages of birth and parentage surmounted, and the life beautified and inspired and energised with God-given powers.

By thought man either blesses or curses himself. By it he brings into his life either success or failure, health or disease, happiness or unhappiness, poverty or prosperity. It is all in his mind and the character of his thought.

Whatever there is in your life or mine, of disharmony, lack, sickness or unhappiness, is the result of our disharmonious thought. We live in an orderly Universe, but we do not react harmoniously to our environment, we are not in correspondence with the hidden law and order around us. It is not necessary for the universe to be altered; what is needed is that we ourselves should be changed.

Within ourselves is the cause of the disorder in our own individual world--for we each live in a little world of our own creation-- therefore, the disorder and trouble that afflicts us, or the lack that restricts our life, can never be overcome, save by a change of mind, habit of thought, and mental attitude.

In the following pages an attempt is made to show how the reader can, by changing his thoughts and mental attitude, "reverse the lever" and come into harmony with the Divine Idea. When this is accomplished, his life will blossom like the rose, "he shall be led forth with peace; the mountains and the hills shall break before him into singing, and all the trees of the field shall clap their hands."

Contents

THOUGHT THE CAUSE OF ACTION 1
VICTIMS OF IGNORANCE..6
VICTIMS OF SUGGESTION 11
THE SECRET OF OVERCOMING..16
CREATORS OF OUR OWN EVIL?..24
RIGHT THOUGHT AND A RIGHT ATTITUDE....................28
THE BASIS OF SUCCESS AND PROSPERITY 28
THE EFFECT OF THOUGHT ON HEALTH 33
THE ATTRACTIVE POWER OF THOUGHT 40
THOUGHT-CONTROL AND SPIRITUAL ATTAINMENT..45
THE OVERCOMING OF FEAR...50
NOT DEMAND, BUT OBEDIENCE 54
FIRST STEPS 58
BIOGRAPHY OF THE AUTHOR..65

THOUGHT THE CAUSE OF ACTION

THERE is the conscious mind and there is the subconscious mind. The conscious mind gathers knowledge and experience through the senses. It learns from books, conversation and experience. It reasons and forms conclusions. Finally its thoughts pass down into the subconscious mind.

The subconscious mind is the mind of action. It is responsible for all that we do. It is the seat of memory and of instinct. It is a reservoir of tremendous power, it is of extraordinary intelligence, it carries out all the complicated processes within the body, which make life possible.

The wisest and most learned of men cannot begin to fathom its wonderful powers, but in spite of this we know enough about its manner of working to enable us to control it, and by controlling it, we control our actions, and by controlling our actions we shape our life, and overcome what is called fate.

The Power of Thought

The subconscious mind, although so wonderfully intelligent and possessed of such extraordinary powers, acts entirely upon suggestion. That is to say, it follows blindly and faithfully the thoughts that are sent down into it. Therefore upon our thoughts depends what sort of actions are brought forth.

If evil thoughts are sent down into the subconscious mind, then evil, destructive action will be the natural result. If thoughts of weakness and failure are entertained, then weak actions leading to failure will inevitably follow.

On the other hand, if good thoughts are entertained, then constructive good action will result, and if strong, successful thoughts are entertained, they bring forth robust, constructive action, which leads to success and achievement. It is impossible to think evil thoughts and bring forth good actions.

Many have tried it. They have said, I will be outwardly respectable and blameless in life, but in secret I will think this thought, I will hug it to my bosom because it is pleasant, but I will let it go no further, because I know that evil action leads to shipwreck and disaster. Therefore I will deceive even my best friends.

Outwardly I will be all that I ought to be, but in my thoughts I will be evil. Mine will be a double life, to outsiders I shall be one thing, and in my thought-world something different. Thus I shall be able to enjoy evil in thought, and escape its penalties!

Such an one does not reckon with the power and faithfulness of the subconscious mind. Every evil thought which is entertained and gloated over, acts as a powerful suggestion to this patient giant, until at last it can stand it no longer, and bursts out into the life in the form of a course

2

of evil action, which is an exact replica of the thoughts which have been entertained.

This explains why so often people who have always been so exemplary in their conduct all at once go wrong, and come crashing down to ruin; they are simply reaping the harvest of their thoughts.

While this is true of the majority of those who indulge in secret evil thinking, there are yet those who, either through lack of courage or opportunity, do not, or cannot, "break out" into a course of evil action.

By their evil thoughts they arouse certain emotions which cannot be satisfied and which therefore have to be re-pressed. The effect of repression is either chronic ill-health which no medical skill can ever cure, or organic disease that is beyond the art of man to heal. The reader must not imagine, however, that everyone who suffers in this way has been guilty of evil thinking, but the practice is certainly one of the ways by which some people can, and do, liter-ally destroy themselves.

This example is merely given as an illustration of the effect of evil thinking, and most people have seen evidences of it amongst their friends and relations.

Most of my readers will doubtless be above this kind of thinking, but the same law acts with every kind of thought that is sent down into the subconscious mind. There are two kinds of thought, viz., constructive and destructive, sometimes called positive and negative.

It depends upon which class of thought we persistently dwell upon and pass to the subconscious mind, what our actions in life are to be. If we allow our mind to dwell on destructive, negative thoughts, and this, unfortunately, is often the case as it requires no effort, then destructive and negative action will be the inevitable result. On the other hand, if we think positive or constructive thoughts--and, to do this, effort is required, just as effort is required in climbing a hill--constructive action takes place as a natural result.

Thus a man who gives way to hate and broods over his wrongs, will be led to think of murder, and if he gloats upon thoughts of murder a time will come when he may attempt murder. On the other hand, if the same man will keep his mind off his wrongs and think thoughts of forgiveness, or, better still, if he will love, or hold in thoughts of good-will the one who has wronged him, then his life will become happy and peaceful, and in its highest sense, successful.

Again, a man who gives way to weak, fearful thoughts, who fears that his business will fail, who fears that his luck may give out, who fears that competition will arise with which he will be unable to cope, such a man will probably fail, because all his actions will be weak and hesitating and lacking in that strength and decision which are necessary for the achievement of success.

On the other hand, if he will banish every weak negative thought, every thought of possible failure, and constantly brace his mind by affirmations of success--in other words, send down strong suggestions of success to his subconscious mind--such a man will succeed in life, because his actions will be strong and decisive.

When faced by great difficulty he will find that his subconscious mind will supply him with wonderful energy and staying power, great courage and determination, simply because it has been trained by right thinking to do so.

It would be possible to fill a book with illustrations of the operation of this law, but in a little work of this kind these two must suffice. The law is immutable: it cannot be tricked or evaded.

Whatever we think becomes sooner or later translated into action; and as upon our actions our life depends, it will be seen that it is possible by thought-control to govern our life. For by controlling our thoughts we govern our actions; by governing our actions we mould our life and circumstances, thus shaping our fate.

Life is not a matter of chance or luck; it is not something out of our control; it is largely the result or effect of our thoughts. Therefore, by controlling our thoughts--and this, thank God, can be done--we can govern and direct our life to an almost unbelievable extent.

As conscious thinking beings, created, the Bible says, in God's likeness and image, or in other words, a microcosm of the macrocosm, we possess one of the greatest powers in the universe. and this power is thought.

It depends upon how we use this wonderful power what our life shall be. The engine driver sends his engine either backward or forward, but it is the same power that is used in each case. In the same way, thinking man can either build up or destroy himself by the use or misuse of the potent power of thought. It depends upon how he uses this power, either for good or ill, as to whether his life shall be successful, healthy, happy or harmonious, or lacking in definite achievement, true success and happiness. "Whatsoever a man soweth, that shall he also reap."

2

VICTIMS OF IGNORANCE

WE do not believe that there are many who deliberately think negative thoughts. Most people mean well and want to do good and be good (not goody, goody). But, nevertheless, most of us are wrong thinkers, more or less, and this is due, so we firmly believe, mainly to ignorance. Because it is not generally known that negative thoughts are highly destructive, we ignorantly indulge in them, thinking that they do no harm.

Actually, thoughts of impurity, anger, revenge, hate, resentment, envy, brooding over wrongs, brooding over sorrows, losses and griefs; thoughts of fear, failure, weakness, penury, sickness, disease, decay, mortality and death, are all highly destructive. They are destructive of health, of happiness, of circumstances, of life in all its departments.

They break down the nervous system; they paralyse endeavour; they undermine the will; they make for wrong decisions. It will be admitted that this is a matter of prime importance, yet neither children nor the general public are

6

instructed in these vital matters. Because of this almost universal ignorance we most of us go on indulging in negative thinking, much to our detriment.

How many of us, for instance, realise that it is thought that kills and not lack of food in most cases of death through alleged starvation?

If a person cannot get food to eat he dies in a very few days, as a rule; yet a person who fasts voluntarily in order to cure himself of some organic disease can do so, if the fast is wisely undertaken, for forty or even more days, not only without injury, but with greatly beneficial results. Why is it that in the former case a few days' compulsory fast ends in death, while a voluntary fast of six weeks or so results only in good? The answer is of course that it is the state of the mind and the character of the thoughts that kill, and not the lack of food.

Again, after a few days' "starvation" a person is generally in a state of great weakness and prostration. Yet one who submits himself to a voluntary fast generally continues his work, and it is only at the later stages that he works less hard than usual.

The certain reverend gentleman who recently fasted for forty or fifty days, particulars of which were given in our daily newspapers, not only carried on his usual duties, but, in addition, wrote a book on a subject requiring great concentration and mental effort.

Contrast all this with the state of a starving man, who, after a few days, is reduced to a condition of collapse and exhaustion, quickly followed by death, and we see how great is the power of mind and thought. In the case of the "starving" man, he thinks that he is dying, because he has no food, and consequently very soon does die.

The fasting man thinks that by fasting he is improving his health, and his health is improved in consequence, even to the overcoming of incurable (so-called) organic disease. There have been reported in the papers lately many cases of important people undergoing, voluntarily, a long fast, and by so doing winning their way to health. But this is not new by any means. To my knowledge this method of cure was quite well known in certain circles a quarter of a century, or more ago; but its mental aspect does not seem to have been appreciated at its true value.

There is no reason why a starving man, if he was well nourished at the commencement, should not live as long as a fasting man, and he would do so if he could only control his thoughts and think in the same way that a fasting man thinks. But first of all he would have to be convinced that fasting is beneficial to health, and this would not be easy, for ignorance and prejudice die hard. Also, because man is prone to look to the future with anxiety he would probably be consumed with worry, fearing that he would be unable to obtain food after his compulsory fast had got beyond the beneficial stage or limit.

But the fact remains that it is not the absence of food that kills a starving man, so much as his state of mind. It is his fear thoughts that kill him, just as it is the thoughts and expectation of cure that keep the fasting man alive and maintain his strength and ability to work.

It must not be assumed from these few remarks that I am in favour of promiscuous fasting, for an ill-considered fast might do a great deal of harm. Fasting in some cases is beneficial, but it should be taken under experienced supervision.

There is also much ignorance on another point, which is the possibility of controlling thought. It is not generally known that our thoughts can be controlled and regulated in much the same way that a London policeman controls and regulates the traffic. He holds up a hand and instantly the traffic behind him stops, allowing vehicles from a cross street to pass instead. Our thoughts can be controlled and regulated in much the same manner, Undesirable, destructive thoughts can be arrested, while other thoughts of a desirable and constructive character can be encouraged.

People say: "You can't help thinking these thoughts can you?" They take it for granted that one cannot control one's thoughts. They do not realise that it is possible deliberately to change the subject as regards one's thoughts, in the same way that one changes the topic of conversation. We all of us change the subject of conversation when it becomes distasteful to us, but how many of us change the subject of our thoughts in the same deliberate manner, by the exercise of our will? Yet it can be done, almost as easily, if we will only DO IT, instead of thinking and saying that it cannot be done. Not only is it possible to change the subject of our thoughts, but it is also possible to refrain from thinking altogether.

Both are accomplishments of the highest possible value and they can be acquired only by practice and self training; but, even the weakest of us can acquire them if we are quietly persistent.

We do not need to be clever, or greatly gifted, or out of the ordinary. Indeed, we may be very much under the average in mental gifts, will power and intellectual endowments; yet, if we are quietly persistent, we can learn to overcome our thoughts, in course of time.

And when we become master of our thoughts we become master of ourselves, and when we become master of ourselves we become master of life itself; not by opposing the discipline of its experiences, but by dealing with them in the best possible manner, maintaining a calm and steadfast mind, a quiet faith and an unflinching spirit.

3

VICTIMS OF SUGGESTION

WE are all victims, more or less, of suggestion. Strong-minded and unscrupulous people deliberately influence others by suggestion, in order to take advantage of them. Counsel in Court says to a witness: "I suggest to you," and then follows a suggestion that may be both untrue and unfair, yet it may so overwhelm or confuse a witness as to destroy the value of his evidence. Thus does a strong mind dominate a weaker by force of will and suggestion.

The hypnotist suggests to his victim that a piece of cold metal applied to his bare back is a red hot iron, and immediately the flesh is scorched and blistered, much the same as would be the case if the metal were actually red hot. Or he may suggest to his victim that a cup of paraffin is a cup of lemonade, and he, the victim, will then drink it, evidently enjoying it and thinking it to be lemonade. Thus in these and many other ways does the hypnotist show how powerful suggestion is.

In one of Dr. Schofield's books, I think it is, a tale is told of two well-known physicians who, in order to prove the

11

power of suggestion, beckoned to a man in a restaurant and then told him that he was seriously ill and ought to be in bed. The man, knowing their reputation and high standing as medical men, believed them, went home, took to his bed and died. It is only fair and charitable to suppose that neither of the doctors expected anything more than a slight illness to result from what would appear to be foolish and reprehensible action.

We are told, day by day, in our daily paper to take so-and-so's pills. We may not heed the suggestion for years perhaps, yet, sooner or later, we may find ourselves either taking the pills or advising somebody else to do so. You see a man with streaming eyes, sneezing and using his handkerchief. This sight suggests influenza to you, with the result that, if you are not positively minded, you may shortly develop an attack yourself.

In a thousand and one different ways we are affected by suggestion. We receive it through the eyes, the ears, taste, smell, and touch. We are victims of it at every turn, unless we learn to become positive-minded and proof against suggestion in all its forms.

There is not space for me to do more than mention other ways by which we are unconsciously affected and influenced by suggestion.

Newspaper and magazine advertising of patent medicines are most potent and powerful mediums of suggestion. We have already mentioned the effect of being told day by day, in our paper and by means of hoardings, to take a certain make of pills. But modern ideas of advertising worthless nostrums and harmful drugs leave such methods of advertising far behind as regards suggestive force and value. Pictures of people sneezing, and of others doubled up with painful backs, can have only one effect, and that is to make people imagine that they possess the ailment described.

I remember when a boy, reading in the papers of that day, long advertisements which were headed: "What is this new disease that is come upon us?" I was so affected that I became convinced that I had the disease, and badly too. I became so alarmed that I would no doubt have speedily become really ill if I had not told my parents my fears. Never shall I forget the shouts of merriment that greeted my confession. It seemed as though they would never cease laughing.

But they laughed me out of my fears, and I have kept a positive mind towards or against patent medicine advertisements ever since.

Many of my readers must have read the late Jerome K. Jerome's humorous account of his experience with a medical work of symptoms. He said that by the time he had finished reading the book he found he had every disease under the sun except Housemaid's Knee. Written, no doubt, to raise a laugh and to amuse, yet containing a modicum of truth, which, if realised by the masses, would quickly cause the nostrum mongers to shut up shop.

Then there is what is termed "mass suggestion". We are all inclined to think the same thoughts as the mob, and to have the same emotions aroused within us as sway the masses of the people. It is very easy for a positive person to sway the thoughts and emotions of a crowd of people. It is difficult for one of the crowd not to be moved with the crowd.

This is why people, who in the ordinary way are sensible, go "mafficking" on occasions of national rejoicing. It is also the reason why people who are peaceable and harmless in private life may, when in a crowd, join in acts of violence and disorder. It is simply that the mass emotion gets hold of them, influencing them so strongly they get carried away.

It is a fact that some people are more easily influenced by suggestion than others. Some are stolid and phlegmatic, and upon these suggestion appears to have less effect. Others, on the contrary, are more sensitive and highly strung.

These are greatly influenced by suggestion, falling an easy prey until they learn to become proof against it. Such may feel that they are "hard done by", and that life has dealt unfairly with them, by making them so sensitive. But they need not pity themselves, for the reason that they have, instead, much to be thankful for, for people of this type are those who can benefit most by suggestion when it is properly and scientifically made use of.

Finally, we come to the subject of temptation. All of us are tempted in some way or other. What would tempt one severely might not affect another at all, but each is tempted in a way peculiar to himself. What is temptation, but suggestion? We need not argue as to where, or from whom, the suggestion comes; it is surely sufficient for us to know that we are victims of it, until we learn how to resist it successfully.

There is no more subtle suggestion than that of temptation. It is so clever it seems impossible to counter it in any way. Even at our best moments, when we would rise to noble deeds, base ideas and motives are suggested to us. If we are not to fall we must exercise eternal vigilance. And it is because of this that we are told in the greatest of all books, by the greatest of all teachers: "Watch and pray lest ye enter into temptation."

In concluding this chapter let me touch lightly on the teaching of those who state that almost everything is suggestion. Their theory is that we possess only consciousness, and that all that forms our life is the result of suggestion.

Thus, so they say, poverty is the result of acceptance of suggestions of poverty: disease, the result of acceptance of suggestions of disease: trouble, the result of acceptance of suggestions of trouble, and so on. To counteract these suggestions, auto-suggestions of an opposite kind are recommended.

The poverty stricken person is advised to whisper to himself, as he falls asleep, suggestions of wealth, prosperity and plenty. If the subconscious, or, as some say the unconscious, mind accepts the suggestion, then poverty is at an end. The diseased person does the same, except that he uses suggestions of health, with a similar pleasing result, IF the subconscious or "power mind" within will only accept the suggestion whispered to it.

All this may appear to be pure rubbish and "bunkum" to most of our readers. While, however, the writer is not prepared to accept such teaching in the above crude form, yet, so he believes, there is a considerable amount of truth in it. It is not, however, advisable to tinker about with the subconscious mind in this way. Many today are suffering from the effects of unwise experiments made without knowledge or experience.

4

THE SECRET OF OVERCOMING

MOULDING AND SHAPING LIFE LIKE CLAY IN THE HANDS OF THE POTTER

WHY is right thought so important? It is important because it influences our actions. It is important because it builds up character and a steadfast mind. It is important because upon it our well-being and the success of our whole life depend. It is important because it is by right thought that we can overcome harmful suggestion.

First of all we have to realise that thought is the cause of our actions and decisions. It is largely because of this that our circumstances depend upon our thoughts. If, for instance, we do not overcome life's difficulties *in our thoughts*, then we can never overcome them in actual experience.

By this I mean that our difficulties must be boldly met and conquered *in thought*, if ever we are to hope to overcome them actually. In a way it is good advice to tell people not to dwell upon their woes but to think of pleasant things instead, but it is liable to lead to a habit of thought almost as destructive as brooding over trouble.

This negative application of what is meant to be good advice is responsible for the failure of those who say: "I have tried right- thinking, but it makes no difference." The reason "it makes no difference" is that it is not right-thinking at all, but actually a form of wrong-thinking. Such people say: "I never indulge in wrong thoughts about my troubles, I refuse to think about them." Just so, and it is here where the whole trouble lies.

Instead of life's trouble being met boldly and conquered in *thought* they are run away from. As soon as the mind comes up against an unpleasant thought, thought of an irksome duty that must be done or of a crisis that must be faced, or of a difficulty that has to be overcome, the mind "dodges" it and hits on to something more pleasant.

The one who says : "I never think of my troubles" and who runs away from unpleasant thoughts of this kind finds that he can never overcome the actual difficulties when they arise. In fact his so-called right thinking prevents him from making decisions and from dealing firmly and sensibly with his difficulties. We must first overcome *in our thoughts*, if ever we are to overcome in actual experience.

The world may be divided into two classes of people: (1) those who overcome life, and (2) those who are overcome by life. Those who overcome life's difficulties are those who do so *in thought.*

Those who are overcome by life's difficulties, are those who do not overcome in thought. If the latter have not deliberately made a practice of "dodging" unpleasant thoughts in an unfortunate attempt to follow a form of wrong thinking which they erroneously believed to be right-thinking, they yet are passive; that is, they fail to overcome, *in thought*, the difficulty that must be overcome, sooner or later, in actual experience.

The secret of overcoming is in thought victory. If we continually overcome in our thoughts we develop a steadfast mind. Without a steadfast mind it is impossible to be victorious in life's battle.

On the other hand, there is no difficulty, capable of human solution, that cannot be overcome by a steadfast mind. Indeed, if a man's mind is steadfastly directed towards a certain object, not only will he be truly successful, but the most remarkable things may happen or be achieved, beyond anything that might be hoped for or expected.

The mind becomes powerful, growing in strength continually, through meeting a difficulty, *in thought*; moving forward towards the difficulty, *in thought*; and then putting the weight of the mind and will behind it.

Then the "whole man" moves forward, going right through the difficulty to the other side, victoriously. This generates inward power, that is cumulative, which, when we come to our difficulty in actual experience, helps us through it successfully.

Now this is quite different from worrying over things. Worry is a destroyer. By worrying over our troubles we not only stimulate fear, one of the most destructive of the emotions, but we also wear grooves in the brain, round which our thoughts revolve in endless repetition.

The brain becomes so constructed or arranged, through the practice of worrying, that worry becomes a habit. That is to say, as soon as a thought of some impending trouble comes to us, or something goes wrong in our life or work, or we think that something has gone wrong or will go wrong, or we fear that it may go wrong, then immediately the cells used by worry are stimulated into action--being already fully charged with nervous energy, waiting to explode--and round and round the thoughts go, along the groove prepared for them. Then good-bye to our peace of mind; good-bye to sleep; and, in time, good-bye to health.

Some people are of a worrying nature. They inherit it from their parents. The writer is one of them. Some people, on the contrary, never worry about anything. If they were sentenced to death they would probably sit down and read a book; if the executioner stood beside them they would probably say: "Please wait a minute or two until I have finished this chapter."

A certain man of my acquaintance had once to be told that he was suffering from a disease that would rob him of one of his senses. "Now," he was told, "you must try not to worry about it." He laughed a quiet, untroubled laugh and then said: "I shall not worry; we are not a worrying family; we take things as they come, and we find they are not so very dreadful after all. There are always compensations."

This shows the amazing difference there is in people's nature and temperament. We think, however, that the proportion of people who worry is much larger than that of those who do not. As the subject of worry is such an important one, a separate chapter must be devoted to it.

But while we must not worry about our troubles or imaginary fears, yet we must meet them boldly in thought and will. On no account must we run away from them, for there probably is nothing more negative and destructive than this.

The Power of Thought

Those who refuse to face their difficulties and who keep on dodging the issue are, generally speaking, the greatest of worriers. Avoiding the issue in thought increases the trouble, therefore there is really more about which to worry.

At the risk of repeating myself I must again point out this most vital and important truth that we must overcome in thought. The teaching that bids you merely to dismiss your trouble from your mind and think of pleasant things, or to indulge in a day-dreaming, can be positively followed, but as usually applied is quite negative.

When applied in a negative way it weakens the will, robs one of initiative, and destroys one's power to decide and act. Instead of avoiding the issue, whenever the thought of the impending trouble or difficulty rises into consciousness, we should meet it boldly, affirming our ability to overcome it and be victorious.

If, every time the thought arises, it is met with an affirmation of power, overcoming and victory, then when the time arrives to meet the difficulty in actual experience, we find that we have ample power to overcome and go victoriously through the experience. We find ourselves steadfast in mind and possessed of a reserve of power that surprises us.

Meeting thoughts of failure, difficulty or fear in this way has an effect upon the subconscious mind. It receives a definite lead and realises what is expected of it. Being a faithful servant it does not fail us.

These affirmations may be of various kinds and must of necessity vary according to the type of person using them. To one no affirmation that is not scriptural and devotional in character can be of any assistance.

To another a "religious" type of affirmation would not be helpful, but a more psychological form might be satisfactory. Each must choose that form that appeals to him. One who starts with a psychological form of affirmation may finally adopt a religious or devotional one. The form that appeals to one "at the present time" is the right one at the present time.

When, therefore, the religiously-minded person encounters a thought of difficulty, trial or fear he can meet it boldly with the counter thought or affirmation: "I can do all things through Christ who strengtheneth me, therefore I will go right through this trouble in the power of Christ which is mine to use now and always."

At the same time he can picture himself going through his difficulty with a push, being carried along by invisible powers. In course of time a mental habit is formed of meeting all difficulties and fears mentally with a victorious push. Instead of running away from them in thought, they are met, naturally and habitually, by a "feeling" of victorious push. One who does this becomes very strong, steadfast, persevering, persistent and "big" in character.

Another type may not be able to use the religious form of affirmation, but he may use something similar but in a different form. He may meet the thought of trouble or fear by merely repeating the words: Success, victory, overcoming; at the same time picturing himself going through his trouble or difficulty triumphantly, sustained and strengthened by powers he does not understand, but which well up within him.

Through cultivating this habit of mind the life becomes greatly changed, simply because the character is improved out of all knowledge. Instead of life's difficulties overwhelming him, the student overcomes them. When he has achieved this victory he finds fresh fields to conquer, new and beautiful vistas opening before him. He finds that he can mould and shape his character, and by this means, mould and shape his life.

Some people think in the form of mental pictures. The nature of their life and the character of their circumstances, depend upon the character of their mental pictures. Therefore, if they are those of trouble, failure, etc., they should be reversed into their positive opposite.

Some people are naturally given to negative mental picturing. When they think of quarter-day they picture themselves as unable to pay their rent, and the awful consequences, such as forced sale, eviction, and so on. When they think of business, if a proprietor, they see a picture of bankruptcy, and of themselves in the Court, being cross-examined by the Official Receiver.

If they belong to the employed classes, they picture themselves as out of work, homeless, one of the thousands vainly seeking employment, and suffering all the ills and discomforts that such a position entails. If they see an accident, they picture themselves as a victim, all mangled by the roadside. If they see or read of a hospital, they mentally see themselves as an inmate, undergoing a fearful operation, or saying good-bye to their weeping relatives, as they pass on to a less terrible world.

Unfortunately, allowing such mental pictures to occupy the mind is liable to attract to them the very conditions that they fear and visualise; therefore, it is of the utmost importance that all such negative mental pictures should be reversed into their positive opposites. By this means, not only are the evil effects of such harmful picturings avoided but the very opposite states are made possible in one's experience.

If instead these mental pictures of failure, poverty, disaster, accident, disease and death are transmuted into pictures of success, prosperity, health, protection from danger and a happy old age, then these desirable states tend to manifest in the life, in place of the undesirable ones which might have appeared otherwise.

For instance, if instead of seeing a mental picture of eviction, or of being "sold up" as a result of not being able to pay the rent, a mental picture is persisted in of rent paid, a comfortable home, with no care, then this happy state of affairs is likely to manifest--much more so than would otherwise be the case.

As mental picturing is probably the most powerful form of thinking, too much importance can hardly be paid to its right cultivation. The effect of such cultivation is to bring about a state of positive-mindedness, a most desirable condition. It also builds up character, making us strong where once we were weak, and able to achieve many things which we were before quite unable to undertake.

5

CREATORS OF OUR OWN EVIL?

Do we live in an evil universe and are we the victims of a malicious and unkind fate? Or do we live in an orderly universe whose underlying principle is helpfulness or love? We cannot help thinking that most of us believe inwardly that the former is true, and not the latter. It is because of this that we harbour subconscious fears; it is because of this that we are pessimists, although outwardly we may appear to be the reverse.

Who can tell what direful effects are caused by this inward pessimism? As I have said elsewhere, a belief in evil tends to bring evil to pass. A belief in failure tends to produce failure; a belief in disease tends to produce disease, and so on.

What is needed is a change of belief, after which a change of thought follows almost automatically.

The fact of the matter is that we live in an orderly universe, but we are not orderly ourselves. We are not in correspondence with our true environment. Our true environment is an orderly and perfect universe. The hidden law of life is love or co-operation.

Rheinheimer the biologist teaches that all through nature, in both plant and animal, health and progress follow when this law of co-operation is obeyed, and that disease and disorder follow its violation. That is, when predatory or parasitic practices are followed, instead of those of service and co-operation.

We have first to believe that we live in an orderly universe and that life is based on Love. We have, also, to believe and acknowledge that the cause of our own evil, or the disorder in our life, is to be found in ourself. The truth of the whole matter is that we are not in harmony with life and we are not living in obedience to its fundamental law.

Harmony, peace, true success, and a care free life are possible only to the extent that we come into correspon- dence with life, with the orderly universe in which we live, and work in conformity with the law of life and the universe which is love, or co-operative helpfulness.

There will come a time, so Isaiah the prophet tells us, when this law will be universally observed; when the lion shall eat the same food as the ox, and when "they shall not hurt nor destroy in all my holy mountain : for the earth shall be full of the knowledge of the Lord even as the waters cover the sea." This ideal state may be a long way ahead, but we who know the truth can put it into practice here and now.

By so doing we cannot fail to bring harmony and peace into our life, such as cannot be described. We can thank Heaven every day that we live in an orderly universe; we can pray every day that we may be brought into corre-

spondence with it; we can think and act every day according to its underlying principle or law of co-operation and
helpful service.

Our first thought in every circumstance of life will be, not
what can I get out of it, but how much can I help? This, of
course, is foolishness according to worldly standards, but it
is really the highest wisdom and it leads to the attainment
of a life of true harmony, satisfaction and peace.

There was once a wise man, who lived in a certain small
town and to whom many came for advice and information.
One day a newcomer to the town went to the wise man
and said: "What sort of people are they who live here?"
The wise man replied by asking: "What sort of people.
were they in the town you come from?"

The newcomer replied: "Oh, they were a miserable lot, un-
friendly, mean, un-neighbourly and most difficult to live
with." "Well," said the wise man, "you will find them just the
same here."

Presently another newcomer came to the wise man, asking the same question: "What sort of people are they who
live here?" The old man again replied by asking : "What
were the people like in the town you come from?" "Oh,"
the second newcomer replied, "they were a splendid people, kind, friendly, and full of goodness. I was sorry to
leave them." "Then," Said the wise man, "you will find them
just the same here."

"Rather an exaggeration," you may think, but it contains a
great truth. Our individual world--for we each live in a little
world of our own--is a reflection of our thought life. We
people it with hate and discord, or love and harmony, according to our thoughts. Our life is filled with evil to the

extent that we fail to harmonise with the Divine Order which is the only Reality.

Life is essentially good, although it may contain many disappointments and many blows. Many of these, however, are of our own creation. Do we not reap, in middle and old age, the fruits of the errors or sins of our youth?

Life is good, although a moulder of character. If we harmonise with it, bearing willingly its disciplines, we avoid much misery and trouble. In other words, we cease creating our own evil.

RIGHT THOUGHT AND A RIGHT ATTITUDE

THE BASIS OF SUCCESS AND PROSPERITY

THOSE who succeed possess a certain type of mind. It is true that they have ambition, vision and driving power, capacity for work, and a strong will. Also they never spare themselves, and, in addition, they seize each opportunity when it comes.

But their principal cause of success is their type of thinking. They think in terms of success and achievement, abundance and prosperity. The life tends, in course of time, to express the type of thought habitually dwelt upon. If we think consistently in terms of success and prosperity, then, sooner or later, we express these things to a greater or lesser degree in our life. That is to say, according to our ability, we achieve the greatest success possible in our case.

We cannot all be at the top of the tree, but we can each rise to the best position for which our particular genius fits us. Except in the case of those peculiar people who think they can do anything and everything, whereas they can do nothing properly, we can all accomplish much more than we could ever believe possible. There are abilities hidden within us that are undreamed of.

Our capabilities seem to increase as our responsibilities grow greater. Life calls on us for higher achievement, and lo! the power and ability are forthcoming, in a way that is surprising to ourselves and, probably, still more so to our friends.

I have purposely conversed with a great number of unsuccessful people. By unsuccessful people I mean those who though sober and hard-working and who want to get on, always sink to the bottom, no matter how much one may help them, and in spite of splendid opportunities put in their way. In all of them I have found the same type of thought-habit.

They think in terms of penury and failure. Because of this, all their actions and decisions, unknown to themselves, are of such a kind as to bring about penurious conditions and failure.

Men of equal abilities are not equally successful. One may appear to be lucky, while the other may appear to be most unlucky: but I am convinced that the cause of the difference is to be found in the mind.

The one has a fixed idea of success and achievement which acts as a centre around which his thoughts, both conscious and subconscious, revolve; while the other has a fixed idea or fear of failure, around which his thoughts continually turn. The one is energised and inspired to successful achievement, while the other's efforts are undermined and his energies sapped by a hidden idea or fear of failure and ruin.

Now, while it is true that one may be born with a successful type of mind, while another may inherit a failure type, yet it does not necessarily follow that the latter must always remain a failure.

His type of mind can be changed. In order that this may be accomplished he does not have to enlist the services of an expensive mental specialist or practitioner; he does it himself, by a change of thought. By changing his thought he gradually transforms the fixed idea of failure into one of success. The attitude of the mind is changed and the thoughts are trained to flow in a new direction.

This, in time, changes the whole man, so that he rises like a cork in water, instead of sinking like a stone: he comes to what to him is the top of his profession, or calling, instead of gravitating to the bottom. He finds that there is plenty of room at the top, simply because so few ever use their mind in a constructive way. He becomes one of the favoured few, simply because be uses his mind as a creative instrument and not merely for the purpose of doing routine work.

It must not be forgotten that true success is based on service. It is only by our co-operative help of the world that we can ever find happiness, and this is in itself true success. Money and fame are useless if they fail to bring happiness and satisfaction.

Service and co-operative helpfulness bring the truest and most lasting success. Combined with efficiency they make us indispensable in our particular branch or calling. Sooner or later quality of character tells its own story. Those who rise rapidly, laughing at such things as service, integrity, etc., generally go down later in ruin and dishonour.

Therefore, our thoughts should be not merely of success and achievement, but of service and helpfulness. We should not think so much of "what shall I get out of it", as "how helpful can I be", for all solid success is based upon the extent of our helpfulness to the community. The more helpful we are, the more indispensable we become, therefore, the greater the reward, as a rule.

Apart from all this, the fact remains that thinking in terms of success and achievement, at the same time maintaining a consciousness of abundance and prosperity, tends to attract these things to us. The mind is creative to a degree undreamed of by most people, and our thoughts attract things to us after their kind--opportunities for achievement and more abundant circumstances on the one hand, or failure and lack on the other.

The inner cause of successful achievement, then, is in the mind. Instead of allowing it to wander anywhere it pleases, we have to train it to think constructively. While others are spending their spare time foolishly we must, on the contrary, compel the mind to think positively in terms of achievement.

We can hold an ideal in the mind continuously, around which the thoughts will revolve, naturally and easily. Constructive thinking such as this compels us to work and strive, while other people waste their time in pleasure. It is no hardship, however, but a great joy. It arouses our enthusiasm, after which every task becomes comparatively easy.

Sooner or later, just when we are ready for it, opportunity comes our way, just as surely as the rising and setting of the sun. The law is infallible. When we are ready the opportunity appears.

In closing this chapter may I give one word of warning. Success is liable to become our master and we its slave. Therefore, it is important that we choose the highest form of success, if we can.

As a rule, however, we have no choice, because our ambition is, as it were, born in us. We have in mind the case of a poor boy with only a country elementary school education, who is now an ordained missionary, apparently an utterly impossible feat for one in his position.

Whether he chose his calling or whether his calling chose him it is impossible to say, but in either case, his life of toil, self sacrifice and service, though it means weariness, fever, poverty and derision by the world, will bring him the truest satisfaction.

He is most truly successful who finds his success in service and in trying to make the world a better place for others to live in. Then it does not matter if his success does become his master and he its slave, for such slavery becomes the highest joy and gives the greatest satisfaction.

These are the treasures that no money can buy and which ever elude those who seek them through the acquirement of riches and fame.

7

THE EFFECT OF THOUGHT ON HEALTH

THOUGHT affects our health far more than is generally realised. While it is true that hereditary taints, devitalised foods, and unhealthy modes of living play an important part, yet I believe that thought is the greatest factor. When I say "thought" I include the emotions, for they are aroused by our thoughts, and yet it is possible to avoid arousing emotional energy by training the thoughts to think along different lines than those suggested by primitive desires or promptings.

Generally, in works of this kind, the reader is told to cease thinking of sickness, ill-health disease, etc., and to think instead of health vigour, wholeness, and so on. This is good advice as far as it goes, for brooding over disease and ill-health creates a morbid condition conducive of disease. It is a fine thing to think of oneself as whole, healthy, radiant and filled with life, joy and energy.

Such a mental picture can do nothing but good. Thus the beginner may say "I am in radiant health" and try to feel like it, and picture himself, mentally, as the image of perfect health and vitality. By doing so he takes the first step towards better health. This, although good in its way, is by no means an ideal method; therefore, better methods should be adopted as soon as possible.

But there is far more in this subject than this. The root causes of ill-health go far deeper. In this little work we cannot go into a profound study of the underlying cause of all disease and disorder, but we can mention two or three that are fundamental and of the utmost importance.

It must first be understood that health is a state of "normality"; that is, it is normal to be well, and abnormal to be unwell. There are three emotional states that rob us of health.

They are:

(1) sensuality,
(2) resentment, and
(3) anxiety

They can be overcome or neutralised by cultivating the habit of thinking thoughts of;

(1) purity,
(2) goodwill (including forgiveness and seeing the ther fellow's point of view), and
(3) rest

Although medical works seem to attribute most disease to syphilis and syphilitic taints, yet we think that one of the principal causes of ill-health, if not of disease, is impurity in thought, or the indulgence in sensual thought, in thoughts of amativeness and similar things.

The evils of sensual conduct are bad enough, but we believe that the evil effects of indulging in sensual or amative thoughts are equally grave and far reaching. The evil, from a health, as distinct from a purely moral, point of view, is that such thoughts arouse "desire", and this, in turn, generates emotional energy. This energy has to be repressed, and this is probably the cause of much bodily disorder.

Now, to repress or stamp upon all natural desires as something wicked and unclean is not the best way of dealing with the difficulty This generally makes matters worse. The only perfect way is to think above or beyond these things.

We must reason with ourselves, pointing out that there is really nothing in sensuality, that it is the biggest fraud possible; and that as far as the higher love of the sexes is concerned, if this cannot be ours, then beyond it all are things more important.

Every young man knows that it is far better to rise early, either to do some work, or to go for a bathe, than to lie in bed thinking sensual thoughts. Must it not be better also for a spinster to rise early and do some gardening or engage in whatever hobby in which she may be interested, than to lie in bed thinking of the pure love that can never be hers? It is the same with the thoughts.

The boundaries of our mind must be extended, we must think above and beyond the things of sense and emotion-- no matter how good, in their highest form, they may be--to the greater and more spacious things that are possible. Surely it is better to think of snow-capped mountains, of deeds of heroism, of lives of self-sacrifice, of the great Universe, of the Eternal Verities, of God's great Plan for man, of our voyage of discovery through time and space, than

than the things which arouse sexual emotion, mere amative feelings, or hopeless longing?

Yes, a thousand times, not only from a moral, intellectual and spiritual point of view, but from the standpoint of health. Instead of repressing thoughts of a sex origin, we must think above them and beyond them. By so doing, we transmute the Life forces into higher intellectual and spiritual powers.

Instead of repressing or wasting the force of life and our emotional nervous energy, we use it in higher service. Thus we become not only healthier and stronger, but nobler and greater, both in mind and character. We also become capable of greater endurance and far higher achievement.

(2) Thoughts of goodwill and forgiveness are both healing and preventive of ill-health. Hate, vexation, the nursing of grudges, cherishing dislikes and prejudices, thoughts of venom, and revenge, all these are health destroyers, as also are anger, rage, passion, and similar feelings.

In place of these it is possible to cultivate thoughts of goodwill, forgiveness, mercy, non- resistance to evil done to us. All these generate health currents: they also help to keep away disease and ill-health, Simply because they bring us into harmony with the underlying *motif* of life.

Most of us have doubtless got a long way past the hating stage. We may, it is true, have no desire either to hate or to injure anyone, but have we given up all our little grudges and resentments? Probably not. We may have forgotten them, but they still lie buried, smouldering away in the caverns of the mind, causing disharmony, which is translated into outward sickness or disorder.

(3) We do not think that any medical man will disagree with us when we state that care, strain, worry, grief, anxiety, and similar states of mind are the underlying, or at least the contributory cause of many grave diseases. Many serious ailments appear after a period of strain, anxiety and suspense.

Even diseases due primarily to alcoholic and other excesses are precipitated by mental worry or shock. In spite of the patients' excesses no disease may attack them until they meet with loss, disappointment, or some anxiety or worry.

Then down they go at once. But those who commit no excesses become afflicted also, in spite of their sobriety and restraint. The worry and grief, suspense and anxiety caused by an erring son; the grief and emotional upset experienced by a betrayed and deserted wife; or the long continued financial worries of a business man in difficulties, all these wear down the nervous system, deplete the forces and lay the system open to disease.

It is not claimed that what we call Science of Thought, or Right Thinking, can enable us to avoid *all* the troubles of life, although many of them are self-created, and, in any case, there is still the fruit of past wrong sowing to reap, to a certain extent, but it does enable us to meet them in such a way as to prevent them from injuring us. And this is a very great gain. Two people may meet the same kind and amount of trouble.

One takes it badly and becomes very ill in consequence, as well as unhappy, soured and crabbed; while the other comes through the trouble not only unharmed, but actually sweetened and refined in character. The teaching of people how to meet life so as to come triumphantly through all its experiences is the most important part of our work. There are very few doctors who do no appreciate this part of our work, for they know that if a patient can rest, relax, let go and be peaceful in time of trouble, at the same time hopeful and positive in mind and thought that such will recover quickly and be none the worse for the experience, and thus be saved from being attacked by any of the many diseases that man is liable to, when his powers of resistance, from any cause, have become lowered.

Right thought then is a preventive of disease in many ways, as well as a healer, in that it brings our minds into a state of rest and peace Fundamentally, the cause of all disorder is separateness from the Divine order.

If we could all become perfect and in complete alignment with the Divine, then we could meet with no suffering or trouble at all. The cause of our suffering is that we are not in harmony, or correspondence, with the internal perfect Divine order. God does not punish us, we punish ourselves, or, rather, our evil punishes us. Evil is its own punishment. Being separate from the Divine order accounts for it all.

The prodigal son was not punished by his father, he punished himself by separating himself from his father's house and wandering in a far country. When he returned he was forgiven and all was harmony and joy. Put into modern language we have to return from our life of separateness in thought, desire, emotions and the affections, to the Centre of all life, order and harmony, and become at-one with it. This means that, first, we must possess the desire to do so, and, secondly, that we must bring all our thoughts into line with the Divine Innermost.

Such a thing would, of course, be impossible if it were not for the fact that one who aspires receives help from

Heaven itself. All the powers of darkness rise up to prevent us, if they can, but there is ONE who has been along this path before us, who was tempted in the same way, yet who won a great victory. "Not I, but Christ," said St. Paul, and this is the secret of successful thought control.

THE ATTRACTIVE POWER OF THOUGHT

THERE are two old proverbs which are well known and often quoted, but whose profound psychological importance is not perhaps fully appreciated. They are these: "Birds of a feather flock together," and "You can tell a man's character by the company he keeps."

The source of this attraction is largely in a man's thought. If we think thoughts of a certain type, then we attract to ourselves people of a similar type of thought. We are drawn together by the invisible forces of attraction. It is true that the character of our thoughts becomes, in course of time, written on our face, so that all the world can see if we are pure or filthy, strong or weak, loving or hard, noble or base; but it is largely the attractive power of thought that draws people to us.

Our thoughts not only attract people to us after their kind, but they also attract other thoughts after their kind, and also opportunities and circumstances.

The human mind, although in one sense it can be called creative, is more of a receptacle of thought than a generator of the same. We have as it were, two doors to our mind, one opening to a stream of heavenly, good, beautiful, ennobling, healthful and wholesome thoughts; the other opening to a stream of undesirable, weakening, destructive thoughts. It is impossible to have both of these doors open at the same time.

When we think thoughts of purity, wholeness, charity, etc.--in other words, thoughts of a Heavenly character--then the door to Heaven and all that is beautiful is opened, allowing a flood of similar thoughts to enter.

This is why prayer is so valuable. Prayer is the raising of the thought and attention, also the heart and affections, to Heaven. In response there is a return flow or influx of Divine life, thought and ideas. One who perseveres in this practice becomes, in course of time, so changed by this Divine influx as to be heavenly minded.

Then the other door leading to all that is undesirable remains shut always. During the transition stage, the door leading to evil thoughts may be burst partly open, leading to what we know as temptations. If we try to shut the door and fight the attacking forces, or thoughts, or suggestions of evil, we find that it opens even wider.

The only way of dealing with the situation effectively is to raise the thoughts, attention, mind and heart to the Good and Heavenly Reality. When our attention is fixed in this way upon Reality or Heaven, God or Christ, then the other door becomes shut again.

The only reason for it being burst open is that our attention on the Good and Pure becomes weakened at times. The influx from the Divine, however, continually strengthens and changes us, so that it becomes increasingly possible to keep our thoughts on a Heavenly plane; and this, in turn, keeps the other door more effectively shut.

The negative aspect of all this is that if we allow the door of weak or evil thought to open, the door of Divine Good becomes closed. Heaven, in spite of all its good intentions and desires, cannot help us if we allow out thoughts and attention to be engaged by lower things.

Thus we see here the value of faith. If we raise our heart and thought above our troubles, then we open the door Heavenwards, so that an influx of new life, power and good flow into us, enabling us to overcome.

Directly, however, that we look down, to brood over our troubles, the door towards Heaven becomes shut, while the other door is opened, thus allowing a stream of weakening destructive thoughts to enter.

Thus by refusing to brood over our troubles and difficulties, and by looking in faith to Heaven, and by thinking of the Divine Perfection or Reality, we are delivered in a double way; first, the spiritual source of trouble is shut off, and second, we become opened to receive a constant stream of Heavenly influences. * * * * *

Not only do we attract to ourselves one of the two streams of thought and influence just described, but we also create for ourselves an atmosphere, either attractive or repellent. This atmosphere, aura or personal magnetism either attracts people and opportunities, or drives them away.

If two men, one with an attractive atmosphere and the other with a repellent one, were placed each in a small business and given equal opportunities, the former would do far more business than the latter, simply because he would attract customers, charm them, receive their rec-ommendations and retain their patronage. He would make a living where the man with a repellent atmosphere would starve.

The same thing would happen in any profession. A doctor, a lawyer, a clergyman, would attract a large following, if he possessed an attractive atmosphere, but would have only a scanty following if he had a repellent atmosphere.

In order to create or develop an attractive atmosphere we must feel goodwill towards those whom we meet, we must be anxious to serve and help, and we must think the right thoughts.

There is no need for toadyism--indeed, this should be avoided at all costs---instead, we must remember that while it is true that we have to serve, no matter what our calling or position may be, yet we are the magnet and that others are drawn to us, not by compulsion or against their will, but by the magnetism of goodwill and inward friendli-ness.

We must also bear in mind that we are drawing others to us not in order to serve our own selfish ends, but in order to bless them, help them and make them happier. There was once an undertaker who was so sympathetic he did more funerals than any of his competitors.

His sympathy attracted people because it was REAL. If it had been "put on" it would never have rung true and he would have been avoided as a humbug and hypocrite.

He had no desire to get business with his sympathy, he would have hated the thought, but he simply could not help being sympathetic, because he had a big heart of love open to all who were in trouble. Therefore, we should attract people simply in order to bless. If it makes us prosperous, we cannot help it, our object must be to bless and serve.

Now some readers will say that the teaching of this chapter is quite impossible. They will say, and rightly, that soon after a man begins to think rightly and aspire after better things he is subjected to an invasion from, apparently, all the powers of evil, and that it seems as though the floodgates of hell were let loose upon him, thus making further progress impossible.

This is true enough, but there is another side to the story which is that the one who aspires receives help from above. Every time that we look up, raising our thoughts to a higher plane, life and health, strength and blessing flow into us.

It does not matter how much we may be tempted, we receive greater strength from our Elder Brother than the power of evil that assails us. This Great One has been before us, conquering and overcoming, and He it is who can and does help us in our efforts to rise to higher and better things.

"For greater is He that is in you, than he that is in the world."

THOUGHT-CONTROL AND SPIRITUAL ATTAINMENT

IN this little book I have dwelt too much, perhaps, upon material achievement; but the principal reason for doing this has been that it is our duty to serve our day and generation and to be as big and useful in service as we possibly can. I do not advocate a selfish success.

Our ambition should be, not how much can I get, but how much can I give, in service and in doing things for the world. Thus the success and achievement that I advocate need not be the making of money or the winning of position at all, for it may mean giving one's life in missionary service, or other forms of self-sacrifice and devotion to one's fellows. But no matter what our calling in life may be, the power of thought and the control of thought are of great importance.

A young man may become a missionary, in spite of opposition and discouragement, simply because his mind is steadfast and his thoughts directed towards the goal of his ambition. Apparently insuperable difficulties are overcome simply through the thoughts being directed and focused upon one given object. If his mind were allowed to "wobble" and his thoughts to wander, he would never achieve his ambition.

It must be pointed out that if we pursue success wholeheartedly, it becomes in time our master.

At first we find success to be a very shy bird indeed and difficult to catch. It leads us on and on, demanding ever self-sacrifice and yet more sacrifice, until at last we find ourselves committed to a life full of responsibility and of comparative importance, from which we cannot turn back or desert with decency. Then we find that success, instead of being our servant, has become our master, while we have become its slave.

It is of importance then that we limit our material ambitions. There no reason, however, why we should limit our spiritual ambitions, for if we are successful in our quest of God, there is only joy awaiting us when we find that success has become our master and we its slave.

It is not generally acknowledged, that no great degree of spiritual attainment is possible without thought-control, the result of thought training. Brother Lawrence is an outstanding example of this. He is the great exponent of the practice of the Presence of God.

This humble servant of God, working daily amongst his pots and pans in the kitchen and scullery of a monastery, found that by training his thoughts always to flow towards his Lord, he became conscious of His presence always. So clear was this realisation that Brother Lawrence found that he was far more conscious of the Divine presence while he was at work scouring greasy pots and pans than when in his cell for the express purpose of engaging in devotional exercises.

This humble, unlearned brother became a saint (although not called one) and a teacher of many, simply through directing his thoughts towards God, and persevering, in spite of their liability to wander.

It is possible for us really to pray if we possess a measure of thought-control. We direct our attention to God and this forms a ladder by which our thoughts and affection ascend up to God. Thought-control is really a fixation of the attention upon a given object and keeping it there. So long as our attention is fixed on God, just so long will our thoughts travel up the ladder thus set up.

Those whose powers of attention and thought-control are so weak as to be almost entirely lacking should repeat prayers. This is not as good as praying oneself, but it is a beginning and a step in the right direction. One who "says" or repeats his prayers, night and morning, possesses a connecting link between himself and Heaven that others who never make any such attempt lack.

 But really to pray by directing the attention and thoughts toward God is a very different thing. It is a much greater thing; it is a spiritual exercise of the highest order. It is not an easy thing to do however, for until our thoughts have become disciplined they wander away.

The cares of life, or its ambitions, lure our thoughts away so that we soon find ourselves thinking of things material, instead of things spiritual. Our thoughts must, of course, be brought back again and again, until a habit is set up which then makes real prayer possible.

The Power of Thought

There are many grades of real prayer. There is supplicatory prayer; there is the prayer of praise and thanksgiving; there is the prayer of meditation; there is contemplation. The last two are very advanced. They become possible only when an almost perfect degree of thought-control has been developed.

It is not only during times of prayer, however, that thought-control is needed in the pursuit and development of spiritual faculties and powers. We need it just as much during the day when engaged in the "mud and scum of things". We too can share the experience of Brother Lawrence, who found that his work which he disliked, in the ordinary way, became enjoyable because of the Divine presence. Tasks, also, which before were difficult and beyond his powers became possible of accomplishment when once he had learnt to let the Lord help him with His presence.

By frequently turning our thoughts and aspirations to the Divine Innermost we become greatly helped and strengthened. Also, in course of time, our work which we may dislike in itself, becomes transformed and made enjoyable, through a realisation of the fact that it is a service of love to our fellows. We become conscious of a new fellowship and companionship. We are not alone, for there is One with us helping to make life a nobler thing, to become more faithful workers and servers, to do things from a higher motive.

The result of all this is that a new and finer character is built up, and this is eternal, for character can never die. And, in addition, we become entirely new creatures. We may not be religious, as generally understood, or sanctimonious, but we can become nobler, truer, finer types of men and women, for whom the world will have cause to be thankful.

The inner, or spiritual, life is a very real thing. Two people may become spiritually awakened, and through it may desire to live a nobler and higher life. One may be successful while the other may after a hard fight go back to his old life. The reason is that the former keeps alive the flame of his inner life, while the latter allows it to go out.

The former perseveres with real prayer and directing his thoughts to God, raising them continually to higher and better things; while the latter neglects his praying, does not persevere in the control of his thoughts, so that his spiritual life withers away and becomes dead through lack of nourishment.

Then temptation comes in like a flood and the battle is too much for one who is not fortified by prayer. He gives in and goes back again to the same old hopeless life, simply because it does not seem possible to do anything else. The fault is not that temptation is too strong but that he cuts himself off from the One Source of infinite Power through his neglect of prayer, and his lack of perseverance in thought-control.

The importance of training the thoughts to turn away from unworthy things to the things that are noble, true, beautiful and really worthwhile is so great, is it any wonder that I write books and publish a magazine on the subject?

10

THE OVERCOMING OF FEAR

FEAR is probably the cause of more of the mishaps of life than we imagine. A special protection seems to shield those who are absolutely without fear. It is a well-known fact that a dog will not attack one who is completely unafraid of him. My own limited experience of sports is that if one is entirely without fear, then the more reckless one may be, the more likely is it that one comes off without even a scratch.

It is my belief that the lions in the den into which Daniel was cast were unable to hurt him, simply because he was without fear. It was only necessary for the Lord to take away entirely his fear, in order to make Daniel perfectly safe. Proof of this is to be found in the experience of missionaries. When they have faced mobs of armed cannibals, thirsting for their blood, fear has been taken away from them so utterly and completely, that to advance unarmed towards what seemed certain death was just as easy as meeting a flock of lambs, or attending a prayer meeting. In no such case was the missionary harmed.

But an entire absence of fear is not only a protection from mishaps in dangerous sports, from fierce animals and murderous men, it is also a protection from infection and contagion.

Napoleon visited those sick of the Plague in order to show others that the disease could not affect one who feared it not. I once knew a man who used to visit smallpox and plague hospitals, but who never contracted either disease, although he used to kneel down and pray by the patients' bedsides, inhaling microbes by the million. His only safe-guard was his thought: he refused to admit that the microbes could harm him; in other words, he trusted in God, and so was entirely without fear. He demonstrated the absolute truth of the 91st Psalm.

Thus we see that in one sense it is not microbes that cause us to fall a prey to epidemic diseases, but that a thought of fear is the deciding factor. Two people are ex-posed to the same infection.

One contracts the complaint, the other is unaffected. Why? You may say that the one who escapes is more robust and hardy, but this is not always so, for frequently the strong are taken and the weak are left. You may say, further, that the one who escapes possesses greater powers of resis-tance. Just so, but is not this largely due to the mind? It is the one who is most positively minded who is immune.

Granted then the necessity for and desirability of, an ab-sence of fear, how are we to overcome our hereditary failing? Most of us harbour fear of some kind; for although fearless in some things we may yet have other fears lurk-ing in the hidden caverns of our mind.

The Power of Thought

We may be physically brave and yet have fears for our business, our profession, or our employment. The gaunt spectre of unemployment, of bankruptcy, of failure to make good, may haunt us night and day.

On the other hand, we maybe unafraid of these things, yet fear disease, infection, contagion, draughts, etc., so that every fresh epidemic fills us with apprehension and dread. How then are these fears to be overcome? In exactly the same way as you would calm the fears of your little child who might awaken during the night and be afraid of the dark.

You would first say "There is nothing to be afraid of." You might then reason with them, showing him that the room is just the same when it is dark as when it is illuminated, and that the things he fears are merely in his own mind. Then if this is not sufficient you say: "I will stay with you and will hold your hand so that you will know that everything is all right, and that there is nothing to fear." Feeling your presence with him, and being quite certain of your power and willingness to protect him, he soon falls quietly to sleep.

Now we have to treat ourselves in exactly the same way. We are very complex creatures and can actually speak, argue, and reason with our own selves. We proceed in exactly the same way as we did with our little child. First of all we say to ourselves: "There is nothing in all the Universe that can make me afraid." This is not a mere empty boast, it is a statement of Truth.

We do not mean by this that we, ourselves, are so strong that we can meet and overcome all the powers of evil. What it means is that we, having put ourselves on the side of the angels the angels have put themselves on our side, in response, so to speak.

Overcoming of Fear

It means we have come into alignment with the inner harmony of the Universe. The Divine Order which nothing can
destroy, and over which the forces of disorder have no
power whatever. It means that behind us is all the power of
hidden Divine Forces pushing us on to the glorious con-
summation designed and planned for us in the depths of
the Divine Mind and the Heart of Infinite Love.

Therefore, we can next use the words of Edward Carpen-
ter: "All the Divine Forces hasten to minister to my eternal
joy." While doing this we can feel and realise that it is just
as we state; that there are actually Divine Forces behind
us pushing us forward to a fuller and richer life, and raising
us to higher and better things.

If you find these statements or invocations too advanced,
high down or "fantastic" for you, you can quite easily
choose words of your own that will be effective in your
case. But the same process should be followed. It is better
first to use the negative and next the positive.

But, like our imaginary little son who was afraid of the dark,
we may feel the need of something more. He wanted us to
stay with him and hold his hand, so that he might feel and
realise that we were with him to protect and guard. In the
same way we can call upon and realise the Presence of
the Omnipotent and Eternal.

There is One who has overcome the world and beaten all
the powers of evil, who has glorified His humanity and
opened up the Way for us by His own self-sacrifice, and
He has said: "I will not leave you," and "Lo, I am with you
alway, even unto the end."

53

11

NOT DEMAND, BUT OBEDIENCE

THE beginner might think, quite naturally, that having discovered the immense power of thought, all that he has to do is to make use of it according to his own sweet will. There is probably no greater error than this. It is because thought is so powerful, and its effects so far-reaching, that makes it important that we train our thoughts to correspond to the inner laws of the universe. We each form part of one complete whole.

God is our Father or Centre and every man our brother. We are servants one of another. Until we realise this we are out of harmony with life and the universe, not only in our actions but in our thoughts; for, if we have a wrong idea of life, then all our thoughts must naturally be wrong also.

It has been said that we can conquer Nature only by obeying her laws. It is equally true that we can overcome life only by obeying the laws of life.

If we do not think in harmony with the *motif* of life we become plaque spots in the Cosmic body. It is only when we become brothers of humanity, living in harmony with the laws of life and the great scheme of things, it is only then that we can experience harmony ourselves, and it is only then that our life can become really and truly successful, in the highest sense of the word.

It is possible to make demands upon life and to get what one demands. This leads to achievement, won of course at the cost of hard work and sacrifice. We have all to pay for our achievements.

Those who are not willing to pay are not able to achieve. It is because achievement demands so much of us in the way of character--patience, perseverance, steadfastness, sacrifice--that makes it valuable as a builder of character. To keep one's success and to remain unspoilt by it demands yet greater qualities of character than does its achievement. But all such achievement can bring neither happiness nor harmony if it is demanded from life selfishly, without any thought for others, without any thought of God.

No happiness, peace or harmony can ever result from making selfish demands upon life. It is true that there is a time in our life when it seems that everything is in our own hands, and that we are master of our fate, captain of our soul.

This may spur us on to achieve and conquer, and to meet with experiences that are a necessary preparation for greater things. All this is good as far as it goes, and may be a very necessary phase in our life, but sooner or later we realise that, although in one sense we are master of fate, in that we can choose either good or evil, yet, all the time, "there is a Divinity that shapes our end, rough hew it though we may".

There is an internal harmony to which we must correspond. We belong to a complete whole, in which we have a place, and of which we form a part: we can come into correspondence with the harmony of this "whole", only by becoming less selfish and more universal. In other words, we have to love God, and love our neighbour. Instead of forcing our will upon life: instead of making ourselves a centre around which everything else must revolve: instead of demanding and compelling, if we would find real happiness and true satisfaction at all, we must love and serve God and man, life and the world, and thus enter into the harmony of the Whole.

The inner law of life is love, but it is better for us to think of this as co-operation. To the extent that we think, work, act and feel in correspondence with this law, do we find true happiness, peace, satisfaction and the things which are precious above rubies and which no wealth can buy.

We see, then, why we should train ourselves to think thoughts of goodwill, instead of those of hate and resentment; of co-operation instead of selfish acquisitiveness; of service rather than personal gain. It is only thus that we can become brothers of humanity: it is only by becoming brothers of humanity that we can ever enter into correspondence, or a state of at-one-ness, with the internal harmony that is Divine.

We live in an orderly universe, for behind the disorder on the surface of life is an internal Divine Order. This Divine Order would find expression externally if every man were to come into harmony with it. But "self" stands in the way. Love, good-will, co-operation, these form the key by which man individually can find entrance to this inner harmony and order; and which by reason of his own entrance he can make it easier for his brother to find entrance also.

There is psychology being taught today, mostly in books from America that is hurtful and malicious. It teaches the misuse of mind power by means of suggestion. The mind and will are used to compel others to act as desired by the "operator". For instance, a salesman wants to get an order from a buyer of a certain house. While the latter is considering the matter the salesman uses strong mental suggestion that the buyer should sign the order.

Unless the buyer is acquainted with this sort of thing he may be compelled to act against his better judgment. This practice of mental coercion is really criminal, although at present not legally so. It is practised in a variety of ways, but the one who suffers most is the one who practise the method and not his victims.

Nemesis awaits all who misuse their mind powers in this way. We can never work against the laws of life without suffering for it very severely. Such mental malpractice as I have described is in complete opposition to the inner law of co-operation already mentioned; therefore it brings disorder and suffering in its train.

FIRST STEPS

"Who hath despised the day of small things" (Zech. 4: 10)

WE cannot become adepts in right thinking and thought-control all at once. We all have to grow from small beginnings, gradually increasing in strength and stature. In other words, we all have to make a start in an apparently small and humble way.

I say "apparently" advisedly, for although it may seem to be a small thing deliberately to think thoughts opposite in character to those which our feelings and natural or lower nature prompt us to think, yet it is really a big undertaking and, if we are successful, a high achievement.

It may seem to be a small thing deliberately to think thoughts of goodwill about one who has wronged us, or upset us, but it is really a tremendous thing of eternal importance. If we merely give way to the promptings of our earth nature we remain on par with the beasts, allying ourselves with mortality, death and decay. But if we deliberately think thoughts of goodwill we step out in the path of liberation and freedom, which has no end, reaching up to the stars.

It may appear to be a small thing to think deliberately thoughts of things pure and noble in place of thoughts of sensuality; yet, in reality it is a great achievement, for thoughts of the latter kind form the very taproot of man's unhappiness, weakness and woe.

It may appear to be but a small thing to think thoughts of steadfastness and overcoming, in the face of apparent defeat and failure, yet it is not such a small thing after all, for upon it the success of our life largely depends.

It may seem to be a small thing to think deliberately of God and things eternal in place of thoughts of mortality and things temporal; yet to do so is of importance for it is only thus that we can enter into eternal life, through becoming at one with that which knows no decay.

It may seem to be a small thing to think deliberately of one's unity and one-ness with the Source of all Light and Life, instead of as seperate and alone, but this also is a matter of importance, for through this we enter into a realisation of the Truth.

It may seem to be a small thing to think deliberately of health, wholeness and the joy of living, instead of brooding over disease, sickness and death; but the results of such thinking are far reaching, for upon it our health largely depends, and without health it is very little we can accomplish.

But while it is true that we are engaged in a great adventure, yet we have to commence in a small way, being satisfied at first with small achievements. That is to say, satisfied in one sense, but not in another. We have to be satisfied if we can at first win seemingly small victories, simply because it is impossible to win greater ones; but in our heart we yearn for greater things, and mean to achieve them when we are strong enough.

The better part of us, which is eternal and heavenly, and which is fed by right thinking, in harmony with the laws and practices of Heaven itself, is at first but a weak babe, so to speak. The lower part of us which is "natural" (i.e., belonging to the lower nature) and the reverse of heavenly is strong and well grown.

How then is the weak babe of goodness and heavenly nature to overcome the strong tyrant of the lower? It cannot do so of itself. It would fail if it were not for the fact that we can draw upon inexhaustible fountains of life and power.

Every time that we raise our thoughts above the things of time and sense to the eternal realms of the good, the beautiful and the true, we open ourselves to receive an influx of Divine life and power.

Every time that we think thoughts that are heavenly and strong in character in place of those that are devilish or weak we ally ourselves with Heaven; and then all the Divine Forces hasten to minister to us and help us.

Therefore, although the new and heavenly nature is weak, and the old nature is strong, yet the former wins in the long run, if we are steadfast and persevering in raising our thoughts to higher and better things, thinking the best thoughts that we can, in spite of the claims of the old established habit of thinking.

Finally, the new nature swallows up, as it were, the old nature, but it is a long drawn out struggle. What we call right thinking is not merely thinking positive thoughts in place of negative ones. It is this and a great deal more.

Right thinking has different meanings to different people. To the beginner it consists in thinking positive thoughts in place of negative ones, together with a call to high heaven for help.

The negative thought and its corresponding positive opposite are the negative and positive poles of the same thing. We can live at either end according to our thoughts. Here follows a negative train of thought in one column, together

with a Positive counteracting opposite, that will I hope,
serve as a key to future right thinking and overcoming.

NEGATIVE	POSITIVE
Thought or Suggestion	**Thought or Affirmation**
Life is evil and cruel. What terrible thing or evil is it that may affect me at any moment? Failure, bankruptcy, loss of employment, work- house, disease, accidents, operation, hospital, bereavement?	**Life is good and is always striving to bring to me the highest good. No evil can come nigh me: nothing can hurt or destroy. The Divine blessing rests on all my affairs, the blessing that maketh rich and addeth no sorrow. The life of God fills me with health, strength and joy of living.**

If you were to sit down and meditate upon the negative train of thought, especially if you were in the midst of a first class "worry", the result would be that your fears would be increased and at the best you would become depressed. If, instead, you meditate upon and affirm the sentences given in the above right hand column you find that you become braced and strong, ready once again for the battle of life.

Not only so, but if you allow the negative train of thought to engage your attention and sink into your mind, then you allow yourself to accept the adverse suggestion, which in turn may bring the things feared into actual manifestation. If, on the other hand, you stick to and affirm the positive thoughts given in the second column, then the evil suggestion is driven out and the positive, life-giving Truth is put in its place. The one who can do this becomes strong and steadfast, while the things that he affirms become, in course of time, manifest in his life and experience.

A quiet time should be spent regularly every day (the last thing at night and early in the morning are good times) in meditating upon the positive thoughts given above, and upon others like them. But during the day it is equally necessary to chase away the adverse suggestion, and in this case it must be done quickly.

The meditation would be far too long to be made use of in the midst of the rush and tear of everyday life. What is needed is a short affirmation that will knock the evil suggestion on the head and replace it by a positive declaration of absolute Truth, Therefore we can meet the various suggestions of evil in the following manner:

Suggestions of Evil	Affirmations of Truth
Disease, Sickness, Illness,	GOD is my Health.
Poverty, Penury.	GOD is my abundant and everlasting Supply.
Failure.	GOD is my success (or GOD Is in me as my power to achieve).
Hate, Resentment.	GOD is Love in me. (Changing me and finding expression through me.)

It is no exaggeration to say that one who will put the above teaching steadily into practice will transform his life, through becoming changed for the better in himself. If our life is difficult and our environment depressing or uncongenial, it is not these that have to be changed. It is the worst possible thing for a man to pray for his life to be made easier and more comfortable.

One who says: "If only my circumstances were different I could get on," perpetuates his misery and binds the chains of his bondage more closely to him. We must never pray for tasks equal to our strength, but rather for strength equal to our tasks. It is we who have to be changed, not our circumstances.

We have to overcome our circumstances and limitations, by growing beyond them. When we become changed, our circumstances and environment become changed correspondingly. We can become built up in character only to the extent that we overcome in thought.

THE END

BIOGRAPHY OF THE AUTHOR

Henry Thomas Hamblin was born at Walworth, London in 1873.
He was from a poor family but very determined and able to rise from his predicament.
It was said that all through his life he had visions of a divine presence. He later described this presence as heavenly bliss where all anxiety and earthly worries were suddenly absent, only remaining with indescribable feeling of love.

After the sudden and unexplained loss of his 10-year old son, Hamblin realized that his life was wasting away and he must fulfill what he was meant to do, a service and charitable work for the benefit of humanity.
He was already haunted by nightly nightmares and this forced him to stop his business practice and retire into the country. He remained there and started a prolific writing career.

His first book was *Whitin You is the Power*, which sold over twenty thousand copies. The core message of the book was the innate power that each one of us has. As long as we are muddled in self-pitty and professional victimhood, there is no hope. It is this belief that holds us back and keeps us down. Once this false belief is shattered, all becomes possible once again. This message is as timely today, as it is true.

To find out about other books, CDs and DVD's please check out our web site;

http://www.andras-nagy.com

www.ingramcontent.com/pod-product-compliance
Lightning Source LLC
Chambersburg PA
CBHW060702030426
42337CB00017B/2727